# I'VE HAD ENOUGH OF BEING NICE...

## *So Here It Is!!*

## Carol Mazzei

1st WORLD
PUBLISHING

# I'VE HAD ENOUGH OF BEING NICE... SO HERE IT IS!!

## Carol Mazzei

© Carol Mazzei 2008

Published by 1stWorld Publishing
1100 North 4th St. Fairfield, Iowa 52556
tel: 641-209-5000 • fax: 641-209-3001
web: www.1stworldpublishing.com

First Edition

LCCN: 2008925279
SoftCover ISBN: 978-1-4218-9865-0
HardCover ISBN: 978-1-4218-9864-3
eBook ISBN: 978-1-4218-9866-7

This book is dedicated to my cat Sonya!!

(Oh yeah and Melissa, Joey, Robin, Linda and to all
the comedians for giving me the courage to write)
But mostly Sonya!

Meow!!

# PREFACE

This book is intended for those who have ever drank, smoked, gambled, made fun of the human race, hated their bosses, smoked pot, had big dreams but did nothing to make them happen, thought about doing themselves in, did some occasional man bashing( women, if necessary), but more importantly love cats. If not… then I guess you'll be missing out on some very flamboyant incongruities.

Alternatively, this book is for when you're not quite in the mood for a novel or a magazine article or a short story or even a ten-verse poem and if you are that's alright to. I look at it this way we live in such a vile world full of hatred and power hungry savages, so I composed a book that will bring a smile to your lips. Unfortunately people do not give a shit anymore… that's just the way it is. Kind and considerate people are becoming extinct… to me it's a down right travesty. It's a bummer… I know.  More importantly, the book is for those times when you need that certain something to get you going, like your first cup of coffee of the day, first drag of your cigarette, the first bite of your bagel, maybe even your first glass of scotch. Do whatever turns your crank…lets face it it's a free f**king country! But me I need a lot of coffee to get me going; I confess…I am a coffee addict, "I GOTTA HAVE THAT COFFEE"!!!!!!!!!!!

O.K.…. anyway I had a blast writing this book and my family and friends gave me the encouragement I needed to follow through with it. All I ask is have fun with it like I did.

# CONTENTS

# UNUSUAL OBSERVATIONS

When someone tells you they like you, don't believe a word of it… because chances are they do this for a living.

When life gets you down; eat a bag of chips. Especially the dill; ya know how it makes your mouth raw and sore and then it feels like the inside of your cheeks are bleeding. After that you may want a delightful cup of steaming hot coffee, then by scalding your mouth it won't take the Jaws of Life to pry the bag out of your hand.

Carol Mazzei

Before your time is up make sure you make it a good one; rack up all those credit cards, do an excessive amount of gambling, do the horse-track thing, don't forget to take out a second or third mortgage, get some drug using in there, a lot of drinking of everybody's favorite friend named "Jack" and at least a few cartons of cigarettes. Then if you're brave enough take my hand and I'll show you what "Hell" really is.

When you think the worst has happened, think about it again and something way worse will happen.

Once I had a notion about love… that's all; just a notion.

When someone has pissed you off or ripped your heart out, never stop dwelling on it, cause eventually you'll go mad and then that way it's o.k. to kill them.

When I'm sitting and watching the wind blow through the trees I feel a sense of peace, but then I wonder when the tree is going to snap in two and crash through the window and ruin my lovely creative table display.

When your cat does something "really bad" make sure you give her, her favorite multi-colored fuzzy toy mouse or shrimp; because you never know when you can give her, her favorite multi-colored fuzzy toy mouse or shrimp again. Unfortunate as it may seem you'll probably be at work the next time.

When things have got the best of you it won't get better, so don't even try cause really... you can't be bothered to waste time like that.

☺

Once I had a thing happen to me so I had to think about that thing until I realized something *awful*... I misplaced my jubilant playmate, *"Cyrus" The Ultimate of all Dildos.*

☺

It's so easy to stop and think for a minute, only for a minute though… "I wanna die, I wanna die… please kill me somehow!" But before it happens I just want to try wearing false eyelashes, to see if they suit me or not. I hope they don't cause wouldn't that be a poke in the eye! And right at that moment you over hear your best friend say, "OH… here's your false eyelashes that made you look GOOD, but it's too late now…! "Hey… remember I said only for a minute though"!

Sometimes I wonder about things like… why there are stars and so many different types of coffee, stuff like that. Then I think about hair that's not mine and a porcupine quill stuck on my shirt… hmmm, I wonder?

Let's say one day I inherited two hundred thousand dollars or won it or got it somehow. That same day I would quit my job and then immediately hop on a plane heading for Mexico. Then from there I would change my name and identity not for any particular reason… I mean it's not like I'm trying to escape from the cops.okay… so anyway I'd blend in –like I tend to do and bus tables at a cantina like my Tarot Cards always said I would.

☺

One afternoon I was having coffee with my cousin then out of the blue he says, "How's life… where's the knife I always say." I looked at him with a bit of surprise and asked, "Which would be a better color for my kitchen cupboards… the yellow snap sunflower or the mystic breeze indigo?"

It's better to be alone and unhappy than with someone and unhappy.

When you discover something new about "you", keep it to yourself, then that way when you're bored you can try to remember what it was then maybe you'll think of something else in the meantime.

If I had a decent man I'd still have a decent man but I've never had a decent man.

Carol Mazzei

When life deals you a thing of moldy bread just look at it this way, it could be worse like a bunch of moldy wood in your bed where someone has played a practical joke on you.

I've had people come up and whine to me; "this job is stupid... my boss is a complete tool... I think I have to go poo..." Then of course to make them feel better (like I tend to do) I say, "Well, hopefully for your sake and everyone you work with, on your way home you'll get hit by a speeding car."

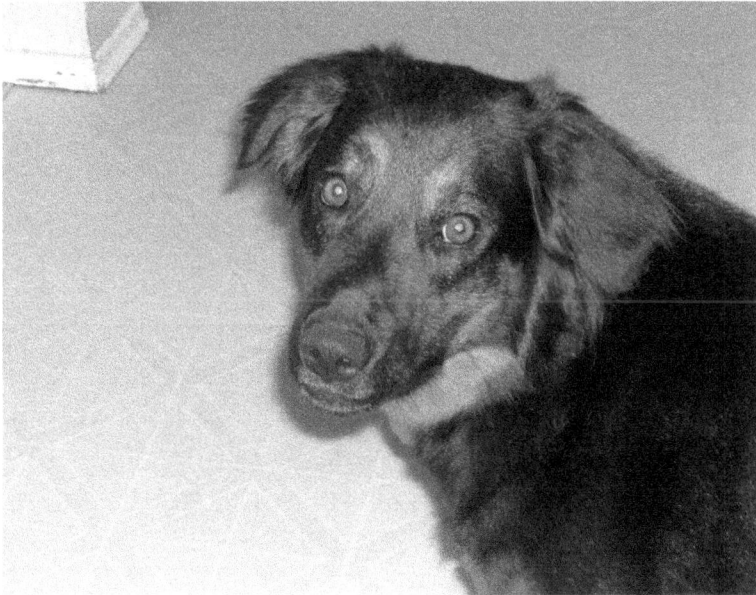

Men are so dumb.

Men are dumb.

Dumb… dumb… dumb.

If, let's say you happen to think you succeeded at something; you could maybe attempt something else, cause you think you're on a roll… but seriously; don't be a dummy. The best way to get yourself out of this ridiculous predicament is to forget about it, undoubtedly that's much easier.

I've Had Enough Of BeingNice... So Here It Is!!     21

When a man tells you something sincere,

take it with a grain of salt... he does.

One can never be prepared when someone has come up behind you and scared you so bad you almost pissed your pants and of course he thinks it's really funny. You could say, "Can you please not do that, it really frightened the living day lights out of me." After that you know he's going to try and pull another childish stunt again. So make sure for the next time you have a can of mace to spray into mister-smart-ass's face... now *that* would be funny!

As life flashes before your eyes, all that means is you were having an acid flash back from the drugs you took when you went to that *Kegger* a couple of nights ago.

The best way to get back at a guy who tore out your heart, stomped on it, and then kicked it really far. Tell him I hope you get attacked by a lot of bats and when you're trying to run away from them, you slip on all the blood you lost from all the bites... which I hope, become infected... When you're falling you hit your head on something extremely hard and sharp leaving you dead... oops! Oh... I'm sorry what I meant to say.... unconscious for days. Oh yeah, all your stuff... it's stupid and ugly.

It sure is shitty when you've been diagnosed with an inoperable tumor, so you might as well make the best of it. Try embezzlement, then some kayaking or maybe even knockin' off a few 7-11's; cause really... wadda' ya' gotta' lose!

Don't you hate when you get into bed and without fail you have a whole bunch of hilarious thoughts reeling through your mind. You tell yourself, "Get up and write it down before you forget! All you've gotta do is reach for the light... just reach for that Goddamn light. Maybe when I'm up I could have some chips, perhaps put in a movie; oh yeah, might as well check the caller's list and make an ice cream float, and don't forget the chocolate. *OH GOD...* I think I just got my gross-disgusting period! Now, what was it I gonna write again?

When the Almighty has finally decided you meet your "soul-mate." He then sat back and laughed and laughed and laughed, gasping and wheezing for a bit of non-polluted air from laughing so hard, said "Oops! Did I forget to mention he's married."

Carol Mazzei

I've Had Enough Of BeingNice... So Here It Is!! 25

It's great when Halloween comes around. Don't dread it like everyone else does, just play lots and lots of cruel tricks, whoever you do them to… they're clueless anyways. Make sure you let your cat in on it too; people are scared of cats… especially black ones with a nice rhinestone collar. Preferably blue, it really enhances the black.

When a man doesn't get his way all that means is that he forgot to lie, cause by lying he has a better chance at getting laid or whatever else he needs to get.

When you happen to think you couldn't possibly sink any lower as a person, just give it a little more time and don't worry too much more about it… Remember, things have their own way of working themselves out.

Ya know that old saying, "If you feed you're…" no… "The great thing about suicide…" no… " If sex becomes all you" … no… "If you never get any phone calls you might as well slit your throat. I mean, for God sake's c'mon… think about it!"

When people make up excuses for everything it only means they're lazy-ass people, who probably couldn't talk their way out of a situation like being held at gun point or perhaps trying to negotiate a deal with some kinda mob guy, ya know… something along those lines.

I seriously thought how much easier life would be if I were a man, cause number 1; I wouldn't have to worry about feelings getting in the way, cause I'd have none and… oh yeah, feelings… oh right I mentioned that one already. O.K. I guess that about does it. Ahhhhh… to be a ruthless bastard.

Temptation is one of our biggest flaws. I think my mind is finally going, can't seem to concentrate on any one thing. Look… my cat is playing with the mat, now the straw, now the mat, now the straw, now her food. I think I need a coffee, god… men are ridiculous!

How is it the saying came about, "You're normal"? What they're really saying is, "You are the most abnormal person ever!" What? … Do you think they're going to hurt your feelings, shatter your dreams, destroy all your mix-tapes you worked so hard at, or perhaps crush your self-esteem, make you wanna' kill yourself ? Maybe, but they can't take away your little dog named Taffy.

Carol Mazzei

It sure is special when Christmas comes around, that Yule-time feeling, decorating the tree and everything in sight, big feasts, the get-togethers, don't forget the bloody gift exchange! You know *how* important that is! If you don't, you're nothing but the scum of the earth, and the rumors start spreading like one big nasty fire that has raged out of control. Of course you don't want this shit to get any worse than it already is. So you run out and buy the damn gift... so they shut up, but all-in-all Christmas sure is... like they say... *"Best time of the year!"*... Where the hell did I put that! @?@!!? Meat clever!

It sure is unexpected, just a down-right nice surprise when you come home and your cat is dressed in your evening gown, and the Bat-phone rings and you've gotta go save the world!

☺

Just when you think your day is going smoothly, don't be a fool… cause it's ruined in a matter of minutes when all your boss has to do is look at you and  insults ooze from his every pore!

☺

Men happen to have one flaw… being alive. And to top it all off they smell… especially the old ones.

☺

I hate it when people say that I blend in with others. It just can't be true! After that I ponder and dwell upon it for days, going over and over in my head... why would they want to hurt me like that? What the hell did I ever do to deserve to be treated in such an awful stereotyped way-thing or whatever it's called! Sometimes I think where does time go when you're eating peanuts, drinking beer and smoking cigarettes? I guess it all depends on how you look at it. I don't know exactly what it means, but there's gotta be some truth to it. It's a great way too muddle through your day. When you can't find anything else to do, wadda' better way than to drink beer, smoke and eat peanuts. While you're doing that, you could ponder all of life's possibilities, like how you wanted to be a showgirl in Vegas and do anybody... *Oh* heavens to Betsy... what I actually meant to say, "Anything, anything, not anybody to get to the top. Who am I kidding ... do whatever turns your fucking crank!

When you've had enough of those customers called, "The Extremists". The one's that will freak out over a lousy seven cents, then makes excessive amounts of phone calls about an enviro charge cause they couldn't seem to get it the first, second or third time and I might add their brain is the size of a spec of dust. But those Mr. Extremists don't stop there, they must tape all there phone calls. So now we'll call them Mr. Paranoid-Extremist. By making these phone calls in hopes to stir up some shit, cause that's there soul purpose in life. This is when you want to say, "Hey man ... act your age, not your frickin' shoe size." These people I'm referring to are known as *"The Freaks of Nature."*

Whatever happened to those women who were women? The Emily Bronte's, Johanna Lindsay's, Tina Turner's, Sarah Jessica Parker's and Mother Theresa's. These women gave each of us ideas, the encouragement to make something of our lives. Now all it's about is who has the bigger penis. Somewhere along the line we have been put into a situation to develop one! I'm not saying there weren't great men as well, but nevertheless men have turned into their world! So women have learned to retaliate and fight for what is theirs but not to lose their identity as women. Unfortunately some women won't let go of their penis… maybe they like it, but I couldn't stand that thing dangling between my legs, so I got rid of it!

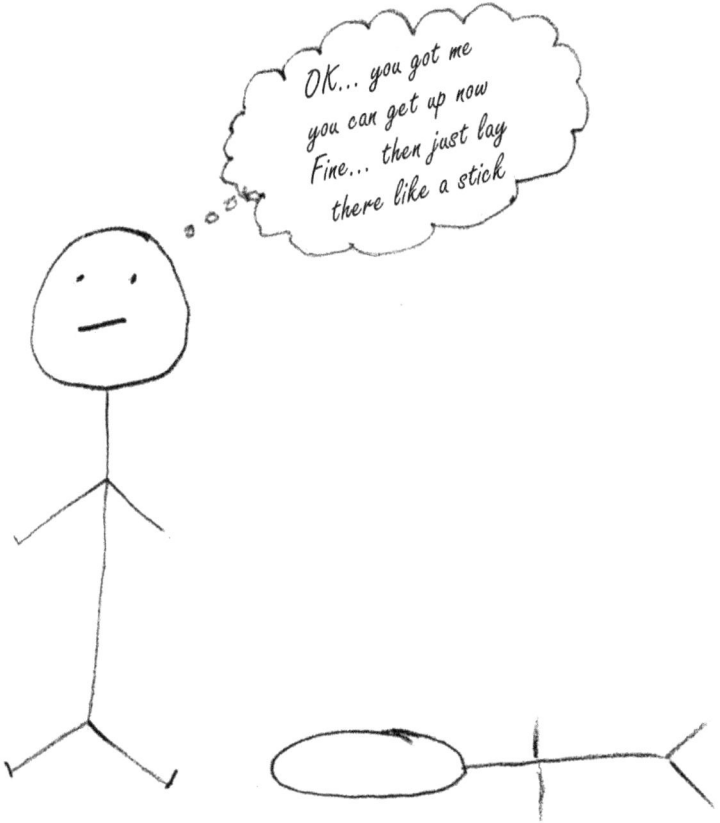

Carol Mazzei

I can't believe when it happens and I hate it, or I don't like it very much; when you're trying to write something and your mind goes blank. Like an empty chalk board, or a piece of paper with nothing on it, a binder that's never been opened, a day timer by no means been filled in, a journal that's never been bought, a white board with the shrink-wrap still on it, a ledger with no entries, a will that's only been briefly thought about, a banjo out of tune. Wait! That's something that goes somewhere else... I could go on, what's the point. What is the point?

☺

There are a few things that bother me in life: the fact that we pay wwwwwwwway too much taxes, and when you have that annoying insane feeling that runs through you, or when people get you to trust them and the first chance they get they stab you in the back. (FUCKERS!) Another would happen to be your boss riding your ass from the time you walk in the door until the time he leaves and of course denies the whole thing. There's lot's more, but I'm going to play with my cat. I think she wants to because she's clawing my head?

☺

Wouldn't it be nice to be easily amused like your cat? For instance, you see a pen on the table and you start batting it around, gnawing on it until you end up knocking it off. Then go to the next thing that catches your eye, like a pad of paper that you could lie across and rub your head against. After that, go chew on a plant, and then maybe knock a few movies off a shelf. Would that brighten up your day, or what? Kinda like buying your first gun.

☺

It's kinda oddly interesting to be enthralled with a movie serial killer like Michael Myers, but what if he actually appeared and really did try to kill you? I think after that you wouldn't like him anymore... What do ya think? Or would you still wanna give it a shot and attempt a *fatal* first and only date?

Sometimes it can really be annoying when you come home from a brutality exhausting day at the plant not too mention the two and a half hour bus ride home. When you walk through the door you happen too notice your kids are duck taped to the wall! Wondering how they managed to pull such an idiotic prank. The little bastards immediately start whining and complaining, "We're hungry... make us some sausages!!!" Just when you're seconds a way to go and set up the rope in the basement... instead you catapult towards the fridge, whip out the damn sausages hucking them across the room hoping they'll catch the raw meat between their teeth or something. Then say, "Christ...what more do you want from me?" Its supper idden it!

My cat Sonya sure is precious. She can't do anything wrong in my eyes. Even if she does, like climb the curtains with her big, orange and a little bit of white, fluffy, 20 pound body-hanging on the curtains and bending the rod, I just say in a soft tone "Sonya, Sonnie, precious, don't do that precious. Get down from there my precious Sonya." When she glances back at me with those big, mischievous, gold, innocent eyes I know she's thinking "Leave me alone, I can do whatever I want!!" But what she's actually saying in her own precious way is "Shut up bitch! I'll do whatever the hell I want! If I wanna rip down the whole damn curtains and rod I will!" "Oh Sonnie-precious; stop that Sonnie, my precious girl." "Seriously, SHUT UP BITCH, or I'll put a cap in your ass!" "Oh Sonnie, Sonnie-precious you shot me in the ass! My clever little Sonnie-Bonnie using a semi-automatic! Oh my precious." She's so clever... and precious... and clever... and oh yeah—precious, my Sonnie-Bonn.

Carol Mazzei

I remember a time in my mundane and cumbersome life when it was what you would call a little rocky, a freakin' disaster, a bloody landslide; well hell… A slit your own wrist and get it over with… thing, that's when you do something idiotic… like try and put your life's perspectives into place. You know the one's I'm alking' about, "The deep thoughts". The; how can I change things bit… where did I go wrong and so on. Everyone has thoughts about it from time to time some more than others but what it boils down to is getting your priorities straight. It may be something as simple as getting the money somehow to build that ultimate cat-room you've always dreamed about with the Devonian garden look, complete with a pond and bird aviary or just a 500ml Coca-Cola so you don't have to drink the Rye straight anymore. Damn those deep thoughts!

What's up with those people who used their tragic pasts to make a quick buck? I could name names, point fingers; what for? *YOU KNOW WHO YOU ARE!* And then go on and write a best-seller about all the shit they invented… or not maybe it really did happen; whatever… I salute their success, cause that's what I intend to do. Undoubtedly my life was no fucking cakewalk. Let's face it; the good thing that happened in my life was my kids, they made my life worth living. I know, I know, you've heard the tale before, but it never seems to get old. Why is that? What if I had said something like: the only good thing that's happened in my life… was my cats, or that bottle of  pills, 2-6 of Rye, case of Corona… whatever was accessible at the time. That would be a whole different story, wouldn't it? To those people who used their lives to get rich and famous; touché I say!

PS—To Whom It May Concern… it was my kid!

Sometime ago, in a not so far away land lived a beautiful enchantress… o.k. maybe that's pushing it… oh alright then, kinda mediocre looking young maiden. She wished and dreamed for so many different things for herself but the one dream she wanted most of all was for someday a handsome knight to rescue her from father and mother's horrible, wicked, slavery ways. With desperation in her heart she waited and prayed night after night for the brave young knight to show up, but it became painfully obvious… *he wasn't coming*. She cringed at the thought of hauling out another 50 empty cases of beer bottles to the garage and emptying the non-stop flow of ashtrays. She was also sickened of being groped by drunken men, which only brought back the memories of her catering days at that *cheap-ass* Exhibition. Undoubtedly, her mother and father's wife swapping parties were driving her to set a gas leak in the house; just a small one. Enough to knock them out for a few weeks; nothing major! Snapping out of her wonderful daydream, she decided to sneak away for only a minute though to refresh herself with a slurped. Dreading her return back to the "Hellhouse" that's when she saw him, standing by his supped-up Chevelle laughing and having a good time with his friends. She could only hope at this point… somehow he would notice her and realize that his true love was only a glimpse away. Then it happened… the handsome young knight looked up and their eyes met. What a stupid dumb shit she was to believe in that true-love-crap-stuff! All within a year and a half, they were married… divorced… leaving her with two kids and never dreaming of a knight to rescue her again!!!!!!!!!!!!!!!!!!!!!!

☺

Carol Mazzei

Whenever I think of the job interviews, which by the way is only when I have a horrible flash-back of my pervious... ones... I've had sitting and basically lying through your teeth, telling them exactly what they want to hear! In actuality it's not an interview it's more like an audition... Frank... ly ooops... that was sure a bad experience; anyway, a bunch of bullshit. Maybe it should be called, "Lie as much as you can to get the job to barely get you by... thing." As an employer "the auditions" are based on two pre-requisites – looks and mentality, cause I mean, let's get real; there's no way Buford the redneck with the missing teeth is going to make the audition. Oh... and if it's a man giving the audition you'd better make damn sure you have big boobs, a firm butt and 18" waist otherwise you don't have a hope in hell! That's when he says his famous line, "Thanks for coming, we'll call you". Yeah right you self-righteous son-of-a-bitch, and I'll be waiting by the phone because I've always wanted to work for a *PIG!!!* Wow, and such wide variety of jobs out there too... like housekeeping, fast food joints, retail and the one they say will make millions... The Pyramid Scheme, but first "<u>you</u>" have to pay "<u>them</u>" 500 bucks just to get started! Then they go on to tell you "It's like any home-based business, you only get what you put in to it, so if you dedicate all your time and energy you should be making some serious coin in a couple of years, so with those words of encouragement... give me your 500 smackeroonies and I'll call you and let you know when your first meeting is". O.k. first of all dick-smack if I had $500 I wouldn't give it to you and secondly you can take your pyramid scheme and shove it up your ass! Do they not understand that bills and rent do not get paid on good looks, charm and Pyramid Scams; you need that little thing called a (and I do mean little) steady pay check. Auditions (interviews in case you have forgotten) and jobs SUCK! As far as society goes... man it stinks!

Breaks-ups are hard and simply a down right waist of your precious time on these sick but unfortunate living quarters we call earth. We automatically believe life is over cause that's how it feels. You think to yourself... How could that "Hijo De Puta" (son of a bitch) be so incredibly apathetic especially when they do the cheating and what's amazing is how they try and blame it on you? He would say something totally ridiculous like; "Well... we didn't have sex last week so I just assumed we broke up... Oh, you had your period so I'm supposed to be a mind reader now... Why didn't you tell me?" With a look of pure astonishment on your face, you swear to the Almighty Ices you'll never go thru that shit again! In spite of everything you must overcome the searing heartache including the non-stop flow of tears for days! That's when he decides to strike when all your defenses are down. So he makes the attempt of the get-back-together-phone-call, cause he doesn't have the balls to tell you those false tender words to your face. As he speaks you have a brief feeling of hope searing through your heart... and then like a bolt of lighting the sensible part of you, the inner strength that has been buried faaaar too long, tells him like it is... Fuck off!! Do we as women have big neon signs above us that say, "Please hurt me again, crush my heart and humiliate me cauuuuuse I love it, and please could you drag me through this at least another 3 or 4 kagillion times you fucker!" They always play the game of... yes I will... no I won't... yes I will... no I won't syndrome until you want to smash his face in with a brick! Then men wonder why we become such man hating bitches!

☻

What would it be like without cocktails? I guess it would be like living life as a primate. I mean, you can't even say biblical, during that era they drank a lot of wine... a-lot-of-wine and did an amazing amount of sinning.

Someone once said there are only two sins in the world; procrastination and impatience. Believe it or not these tie in with the other seven ones. I would explain it... but I don't feel like it.

Some women are irritating… I can't believe I'm going to say this… but worse than men. Now remember "some" is the key word, especially the customers. When they want something you better be prepared to magically pull it out of your ass, cause if not you have given the worst customer service… ever! These types of women won't stop there, they'll want to see the manager and want the address to the head office so they can express how terribly they were treated, in essence they won't stop until they've ruined any chance of you getting hired any where else in the city… cause word spreads like a deadly disease. To those women who do that… grow up and if you want to ruin a life… ruin your own!

☺

A really hilarious trick to play on your brother would be to pretend you get your head stuck under the bed and start crying and screaming, because your head has been stuck for a long time. Then your brother starts crying cause he doesn't know what to do being only *six* years old at the time. When you finally pull your head out, cause you think its *fun* to be cruel. You laugh and laugh and laugh and laugh and laugh and laugh for a very, very, very, very long time! The great thing about it is now he's traumatized for the rest of his life. He's your brother and that's what you do to your brother.

☺

Why it is most people rinse their dishes with scalding hot water… I mean you're trying with all your might not to drop the dish out of your hands because it's so godforsaken hot, but you continue to do it! I'm not sure what's up with that, so always have a coat rack by your door, cause there handy.

☺

If I could draw, I would draw some stick people frolicking in a sand storm with their stick kids, stick dog and stick cat. Then draw them trying to light there stick barbeque... to roast there stick weenies... on a stick Sunday.

I'm trying to understand why people ridicule country music when pop music sends out the same shit. "My baby left me; you turned me into a coc-head so I might as well kill myself!" Not that I'm a big fan of country music I just get sick and tired of hearing how depressing it is when in fact all these boy bands, Alanis, Pearl Jam, Cher, Ricky Martin and a bunch of others who are infamous for it. I know you can't sing about sunshine and lollipops, rainbows and flowers all the time. I just think people should cut some slack on those poor country singers. Maybe it's their drawls or that twangy sound I don't know, but it's no worse than listening to buses drive by all day until it drives you to the brink of madness.

A friend of a friend said once, "Smoke... cause it will shorten the sentence." Coming from a crack whore I didn't believe it for a second of course, until one day my life went *completely to shit.* So I invested every cent I had in smokes, I soon learnt that life has its ways of ending it's self... *I mean...* working it's self out.

Cops are down right yummy… well, except the ones with the big fat guts and there seems to be a vast amount of those. But over-looking those eye sores, actually more like revolting, conception of them… Hey wait, doesn't that make a bad name for the buff fuckable ones cause maybe after a time they'll end up looking like the ones I just mentioned above. You know as a buff, I-wanna-fuck-you-look officer of the law that would be a piss off from a cop's point of view because your chances of getting laid would be… Awww… never! A word of advice, don't become a fat, disgusting, pencil-pushing… chunk! Remember, this is not a dramatization.

Believe in what you believe is to be true to yourself, may it be a determined achiever or just a loser at everything you attempt, cause no matter how you look at it… you will and always will be a person who's a failing loser and that's something… isn't it? That's one thing about me I always see the bright side of failure-ism.

What is it with the justice system? They think they can control your life whenever they fucking want... well perhaps they can but it's not right, is it? A good example is the "subpoena." I think it should be your choice if you want to be a witness or not. But no, that's one of the ways they have of controlling your lives, and they say we have freedom... my ass! Yeah... I guess, maybe they do give you a choice, you could not show up for court then they'll have a warrant issued for your arrest... oh frickin' fabulous, what am I some kind of fugitive or what? When the arrest happens, then you're faced with the mortifying humiliation of the strip search procedure. Next is the hand cuffs and thrown into a 2x2 cell with your favorite cell-mate named Running Water. After being puke on and probably a good chance of being grossly sexually assaulted in some way you'll await for someone to bail you out. Or in which case you could go to court to avoid all that shit only for you to sit there for six or seven hours before they call *your* name and then by that time they've set a trail date, which by that point jail may be a strong consideration cause after all it may not be as bad as you imagined.

☺

Carol Mazzei

I once heard poetry has its way of soothing the soul, so I thought, I'll give it a whirl.

I have a voice
And I'm voicing it
I have a mind
And I'm using it
I have a gun
And it's cocked and loaded...
Oops, that's my private notes, anyway...
I have a cat and she's ripping my papers to shreds
I have a heart
And it's being ripped from my chest
And thrown around like an old dirty hanky
I have a soul
But some scary old voodoo lady put an everlasting
Curse on it
I had a dream
That rye and coke would set me free
But that only lead to cirrhosis of the liver
And I died

It's true... poetry can be soothing to the soul.

Picture it... you just get home from a hard days work and you make yourself a fresh cup of coffee and while it's brewing you change into your favorite shorts and tank top cause you want to enjoy what's left of the sunshine. At that point all you can think of is sitting down at your kitchen table and taking that first sip of your sweet, sweet nectar from the gods and first drag of your cigarette. Feeling relaxed and content you gaze out the patio window where in between the two lush green pine trees is.... *A stupid guy taking a leak*, while waiting for the bus!! Shocked and literally fucking disgusted by what you witnessed you yell, "Hey fuck nuts... what the hell do you think you're doing?! Dumb founded that he was caught he stopped mid-stream, zipped up and muttered under his breath, "It's what men do." I'm glad I know this now, its one more trait you can add to their idiotic disturbing behaviors.

Beauty is something we wish for, in our dreams, in our true existence. Beauty is only for the special, the ones who have earned it... the ones who have been chosen. I have an eye for these things... like ... cat's paws.

If evolution has taught us anything, anything at all... don't fuck with it, for it will only backfire and bite you in the ass. I mean... seriously look what happened in Jurassic Park.

Use my brain? Use my brain? Ya crazy!

Things are great when they are going your way, hey? Smooth sailing but when they're not it's like putting cyanide in your pancake batter instead of baking soda... ooops, butter fingers.

Yeah... I believe in fairytales, that the world is full of bitches, I mean witches and shallow and self- centered men... I mean fire-breathing dragons, and politicians... oooh, what I meant to say was conspirators.

After a time of listening to customers speak, for that matter just uttering a syllable or hearing *"excuse me"* for the billionth time, it sure makes goin' home excitin' to polish up that old Winchester... don't ya think?

My favorite is those people who make 7 digits or more a year to your measly whole $6.50 an hour and have the nerve to say, "Why don't you smile?"... Glancing at them with daggers shooting through your eyes... "Why don't you Fuck-Off?"

Having a wonderful day... Having a wonderful day... I bet that would be like being on LSD all the time.

Love is something like a monkey wrench or vice grips... it certainly squeezes the life right out of ya... that's why it really sucks to get involved cause... whether you like or not it's bound to happen getting tossed aside like an old North Star running shoe.

I axe ya... have you ever gotten ta work and all of a sudden ya just wan ta scream your head off... Seriously... I mean seriously go completely nuts... I guess what I'm saying is "Bellevue time!"

People on this earth... I swear to freakin' god are put here to drive you to the edge, so I guess that's why rat poisoning, turpentine, bombs and so on and so on were invented. Hey, want some... "*Coffee*"?

When you really can't stand someone a great thing to do when Halloween comes around is to buy a melon and fill an envelope with ants. Then what you do next is stab a fork thru the envelope into the melon then leave it where he or she can find it... *that would be a riot*... cause they're *ants!*

All of a sudden you would think of the most exhilarating revenge to play on your ex-boyfriend who has made your life a living hell! Collect a jar full of wasps, (just because they are more prone to sting at any given time) and sneaks into his room, oh and make sure you get lots of opened pop cans to put in his room too. Then you wait for him to get home and let the wasps out of the jar and then you quickly escape out the window. You know... cause you don't want the wasps to get out of the room, so they sting him, a lot.

There is a huge difference between an adult's journal and a teen's… Well basically yours would look something like……

"I got up, had a shower, and had some breakfast before I went to that shit hole called work for nine to ten hours. Then came home, made something to eat, watched a movie and went to sleep."

Now theirs would go something like this…

"Dear diary,

Today I found out that Rob has no interest in Nancy, so bonus for me! I also found out that Alicia told Brook that Rob and I had fooled around; I don't understand why she did that I trusted her! Brook told me that Rob also told her that Lynn thinks that he likes me! I really hope so, Rob and I have so much in common. He does drugs, doesn't drink coffee, and those are the 2 things we don't have in common. I wish he would fall in love with me. I wish there was some way for me to find out if Rob wants me, as in he wants to be with me because he cares for me!! Sometimes he pisses me off like when he says he's going to call, don't get me wrong, he always calls but the only reason he calls is because he said he was, he doesn't call to chat he just calls, I really like him, sometimes I don't like the way he talks to me. Why can't he want me? Whatever, I really miss Blake; I need to talk to him sooo bad! I'm worried about him, where is he??"

The next day's entry is a total contradiction…

"Dear diary,

Rob and I are completely over!!! It's all because of "Michelle" an imaginary person; I really don't feel like explaining the whole thing, so I will sum it up. Lynn and I decided to create someone and fuck with Rob's head! Everything was going perfectly, except for the fact that Rob is never calling me again! I called Rob to tell him that "Michelle" was going to call him in about an hour. I sounded a bit pissed off, cause I was in a bad mood, he asked me what was wrong and I told him "nothing", and he kept bugging me so I told him, it was him, I was pissed off cause every time he calls me he talks about "Michelle"… when is she going to call… does she really like me… is she just fucking with me, I could go on and on, I told him that it pissed me off, because he never called to talk to me it was just her!!! He said "fine, I will just never call you again", so I said "fine!", then I called him a fucking jerk and hung up!! This is driving me crazy, I can't get a hold of Lynn, I know I shouldn't care about this, but I do. Lynn is pretending to be "Michelle", so Rob is going to talk to her and I want to know what he has to say about what happened, even if it's bad. I really don't think he is ever going to call me again! I'm still waiting for Alicia to call me back, and Lynn's mom is never going to get off the phone, and I hate not having a double line! SHIT! I was suppose to call Phil. Hey I'm going to try to call Mark… there was no answer. I don't want this to happen with Rob and I, but hey, maybe it's better this way!?!"

And so… and yeah… I'm glad those days are over, that is to say what the hell was she talking about and what's with all the commas?

☻

Carol Mazzei

# A COUPLE OF HOURS
# WORTH OF MEMOIRS

What am I supposed to be doing with my life? What's it all about and what's it all for? Hell, I've come to the conclusion I'll never know. It's all one big mess after another... Where it starts and where it ends, haven't got a clue really but the sad part, it never ends. It is just so strangely screwed up; I honestly don't know what to do. I know what I feel like doing, I wanna go away. I'm tired of doing what I'm supposed to be doing... if that makes any sense.

As I sit and watch the peacefulness of the water, the few ripples that it makes when the ducks swim across the pond their lives are so simple. There is nothing complex—just carefree lives. No bills to pay, no rent to pay, no fucking bad habits. Dogs named Cookie running freely thru the park, not a care in the world. I love freedom, to bad it could never happen, but instead I get stress and fucking pain and all the rest of the shit. Here I sit listening to people jabber on about who the hell knows, undoubtedly there speaking in a different language. I see a phone, and I automatically want to call the power company and arrange to make a late payment. I wish I had a horse that I could get on and ride away someplace, any place but here! I also wish those people up on the hill would shut their traps and go to another hill, or better yet another park! I'm so disappointed with myself; I used to be so passionate about writing, but not any more. My mind is completely blank when it comes towards writing, that's like right now for instance. All I can think about at this moment is going pee! There are two people on a blanket, just talking to one another probably about nothing, just merely wanting to spend some time together.

Relationships are an odd part of life; it requires so many emotions. Why… why does it have to be like that? And right then there was a wasp flying around me!!! I'm scared! I have what you would call Waspaphobia!!!!! Now I must go run-away and find a washroom!

I'm at the benches now and I'm not sure what I'm feeling besides relief. I grabbed a cup of coffee from Tim Horton's and I'm watching these nutcases drive by thinking they're driving the Indy 500 or something, it's a parking lot for Christ sakes! Well I got one thing going for me; I picked a beautiful night for doing this. I just saw Christina walk by. I checked the time when I was in Tim's, it was 7:45pm; It's almost time to take off my sunglasses. I remember when I was a kid everything was one big adventure… that was great! You never wanted to go in when the sun went down. Oh! There goes Melissa and Ryley; she didn't even notice me. Am I sup-posed to be alone? You know cause it's so much easier as apposed to being with someone, there's just too damn much involved. When I was at home, before I left, I felt like a com-plete and utter shit; like my whole life was hopeless—not worth a fucking thing and I don't know why? I wonder if she'll notice me on the way back to work? Nope—she didn't. How can Melissa not notice me? I mean these are considered "Our Benches."

The sun is going to set soon and I'll still be sitting here wondering what's it all about? I've come to the hardcore con-clusion, I'll never know because it takes a lifetime to figure out, and I know I don't have much time left. I really loath my job, but once again I don't know what to do. What am I good at? Ponder, ponder, think, contemplate… OH MY GOD!!!

There was a gigantic ant or something creepy crawling on my sleeve… Fuck! My chest is hurting… gee I wonder what that could mean? As for "Him" I'll get back to that. People are the strangest things created. Everything they say or do is ridiculous! The worst part about it is they keep bringing kids into this shitty world. Fuck… Use birth control! I know I smoke too much, but that's my choice.

What I don't understand is that obstacle race for dogs or I guess known as the "Dog Challenge". The one where the dog has to jump a bunch of hurdles and the see-saw thing, climb the wall and go through the tunnels. The weird thing about this is the owner is all for it! It is just another ridiculous sport like cock fighting or bull fighting. I'm wondering is it just to see how much stamina the dog has or how tired you can make the dog. Could you imagine if they decided to do a cat challenge-course-race-thing? Now this is how it would go… First is the hurdles; if there isn't a tree beside each hurdle with birds in it… then really what's the incentive, why should the cat even be shown it?… So don't even bother! Next is the plat form walk way… That one you may have success with cause the cat will treat it as if it were a fence, but don't expect any record breaking time, cause she may stop and groom herself maybe minutes or it may be hours or who knows, maybe she'll sleep or nap… or just jump down and run away… I don't know. What's next… oh yeah the wall; now unless the cat is being chased by a dog – it's not happening, not even if you try the dangling toy trick cause then she'll just bat at it a few times then she's gone! After the wall is the see-saw, this one is a complete write off… the cat is basically saying "not in a million years! Fat chance! Is this some kind of joke? Rrrrright!" Finally the tunnel… you know if there isn't a velvety blanket or a crystal glass goblet with her favorite flavor of Fancy Feast inside… then don't even bother disturbing her from what ever she may have been doing at the time. So what it boils down to, it's quite funny to imagine the whole thing… huh?

☺

Carol Mazzei

# RANTINGS

Have you ever had to do something but not sure exactly what it is that has to be done. Because I'll tell you why it's the pressure.....all - of - the- pressure.... so....much pressure, everyone....just....shut up! Too much noise.... too many inter-ruptions.....oh fuck....just forget it.

It's the highlight of your day when you blossom, I mean really shine....it's the ultimate high....there ain't nothin' gonna bring you down....baby! Until an old fling finds out where you work and *can't* get over *why* you didn't ever call *him* back after having sex the one time! Should I say any-more?

I just want to scream sometimes....I'm gettin' on my bike and riding away....where ever the road may take me or how-ever long I can peddle before I drop dead from exhaustion. Probably from smoking two packs a day and then only con-templating quitting but never do. Until you think of the idea of riding your bike out of town but deep down you know you can't because you like smoking too much. Waking up and smoking and having a coffee and smoking and going on your coffee break  and smoking and smoking and smoking ....smoke.....smoke......smoke and smoke.

Life has its way of chewing you up and spitting you out so when that happens reach for that bottle of Stoli and get good and plastered!

If, let's say someone wants to buy a toaster oven.....I'm not sure why....but let's just say she wants it for some unknown reason. When she comes to her decision on the one she wants and discovers there is no crumb tray even though in the manual it says there is one. Instead of looking at a different one, she continues to look psychotically for the crumb tray. I say....if that toaster oven doesn't have what you want then maybe.....I don't know....choose a different one....*and move on!!!*

Love is exactly like sulfuric acid once you have been burned you'll never forget it and never let it go either 'cause that's just the way it is, shitty, crappy, stupid, pitiful, pathetic, meaningless, bothersome.....yeah, that's what it is.

It's weird when men think they have done nothing wrong, it's so true about the saying when God said "this line up over here is for brains", they thought he said *trains*. And you know the rest of it. Their mission in life is to screw with your mind as much as they can in as little time as possible.

So P.S. please let them not have anything, *oh alright...* they can only have Chamomile tea for the rest of their ungrateful lives.

Retail (ri:teil) n.1 Sweat shop without the use of sewing machines. adj. 2. Slaves to management and/or consumers. adv. 3. Subject to HELL throughout whole time working for the retailer.

Misery isn't that bad once you get use to it. Ya know like your first cup of coffee of the day....you just got to have it cause if you don't you are in misery!

Confession is what we all contemplate from time to time. Well whatever.... C'est la vie.

# A COUPLE OF HOURS
# WORTH OF MEMOIRS PART 2

Whatever happened to simple....Oh right....I grew up! I think it should be your choice of what age you want to stay. Getting old is just weird and quite frankly.... scary! It's an outrage life has it's way of showing us....as in the human race sorrow, happiness, jealousy, anger, animosity, arrogance, pleasures and egalitarianism....just kidding I just wanted to write that word I haven't got a clue what it means. Anyway life does this to us but really doesn't issue that handbook on how to deal with that stuff, basically we fake our way thought it like a woman having sex. At least my appearance hasn't changed.... thank God.... but I think I may have lost my sanity somewhere down the road. Actually, that's a good thing cause I'm reverting back to a kid, I like it better, I think.... maybe not cause I just wrote like one. Hey in the long run it sure beats being some cantankerous old crone. Don't get me wrong I'm just as bitter and jaded as I should be, but I haven't lost my sense of humor or adolescence.

I'm back at my favorite bench.... well it's my favorite bench for now until I get to that one in Central Park somewhere. God this tastes exquisite this cup of Tim Horton's Coffee....I love it, oh yeah along with the gale force winds that are happening. Maybe later I'll head over towards the park....maybe not....cause I have a bladder the size of a kernel of corn, I swear it's a curse cause if I'm not within two feet from a washroom....how can I put it....I'm fucked !!!!!!!!!!!!!!!!!!!!!!!!!!!!!!!!!!!!!!!!!!!!!!!!!!!!!!!!!!!!!!!!!!!!!!!!!!!!!!!!!!!!!!!

Find myself, find myself oh forget it; it's that life long quest thing you stumble, stagger, strut to figure it all out. Eventually it will just up and slap you right in the face. As for my cat Sonya she brightens my day, lifts my spirits, takes away my dark moods....what am I saying, I don't have dark moods. I don't know what made me even think of that; I may fall into a bad mood from time to time but not dark. She's just precious in her own unique way, that big fluffy whuffy cat. I can tell you I sure am enjoying the sun it's absolutely fabulous sweetie. That show is great! Patsy and Eddie got the right idea....Stoli, smoking and the occasional lay every now and then. That's where it's at! Another awesome show is Sex and the City. I admire those women because they don't know what they want but they're determined to find it. Awww... for Pete sake....Fuck off wind! Now I can't remember what order my papers were in....oh man....stupid shit! That sky is looking pretty nasty, my plans are ruined once again cause of this dumb ass Alberta weather! Oh super....I have to walk home in the pouring rain, ok....let's see.....I feel like a big fuckin' looser!

☺

It's a fucking hoot when you see a person trying to sing and doesn't know any of the words; it's like a Newfie trying to pronounce a word. They'll say something like "yous guys, I wants" but they sure know how to say "gives me another drink"....maybe not. Perhaps they should start from the beginning, I recommend "Tip"!

☺

# SOME THINGS TO NOTE

I have come to a conclusion....kittens are adorable the way they paw at you and look up at you with those big lovable cross eyes....god that's cute!

It's so sad I didn't become a violinist or even a plagiarist....what was I thinking? I just became a drunk who smokes a lot and has cats.... so what of it!

As pessimistic as it may seem, there is always an up side to life.

Old books have so much meaning like your childhood stuffed animals....bringing back the fondest memories of how your parents partied every night and made you look after your baby sister when you don't have a clue how to look after yourself let alone a baby....I mean.....come on you prick, asshole, mother c**k suckin' mother f**kin' assholes....I'm ok, apparently I needed to release some pent up anger. Don't be frightened....keep reading everything will be ok....I fine.... really. Thanks for your concern. I love ya all! Just go back to listening to Suzy Quatro, she's awesome, great musician for her time.

Carol Mazzei

If things get difficult just quit....because I'm sure that's a sign of some kind.

☺

Whoever said "that's impossible", they weren't desperate enough.

☺

Cat and dog people there is a difference I'm not quite sure what it is but there is. It is the way they talk to their cat because you know there is a special way to do it so she'll understand. Your soft tone, your caressing movements, whereas a dog it's more commands "do this, don't do that, don't pee on that you stupid mutt, oh I mean you precious furry little dog". Wait....that's why men want dogs....to command, whereas women have cats just for companions.

☺

The language of a seamstress is quite interesting... "I need a bobbin, where is my different colored thread....not that color *you imbecile*, I need six meters of material.... STAT....OH MY GOD this isn't working....give me those tweezers....I can't stand this, where is Armand to help me with this, where is that iridescence material I ordered............... *GOD DAMN IT!!!!!*

☺

Don't you find some words are impossible to spell like phenomena or phenomenal. What the hell!?

☺

Aren't meadows beautiful with the long grass swaying in the grass and the beautiful flowers with their hypnotic scents that bring you back to the sixties? The summer breeze and the old trees blowing in the wind.... (like the song) and allows you the perfect amount of shade when you sit down in the shade. The beautiful flowers under the weeping willow trees until it hits you and you look at the trees that aren't so wispy, their deadly, with their bugs festering all over the place. *Oh Criminy!* Giant ants crawling on my fragile legs! *Oh Shit...* spiders on my head....get me the hell out of here....*Oh Christ* locusts....this is no paradise! *I gotta get out of here!*

There is nothing more exhilarating then having your first drink of the day. But it's extremely difficult to settle for only one. It's not a crime that you wanna drink and then drink and drink and then have another drink and then drink some more and after that get up(if that's possible) and mix another drink....and then maybe have another drink and then you could have an inkiddy dink and then other jinkity smiky.

What! I'm pregnant! What the hell... it's impossible! This is just fucking perfect, now what in the Sam hill am I going to do? Oooooh right....I just remembered ....I need to go to the store cause I need some stuff and I can't forget to pick up my suit from the dry cleaners and if I don't run out of time I might make it to Liquor World before it closes... Holy shit I'd better haul ass!

The job industry is such a rip off! You know those types of jobs I'm referring to, the ones that pay a measly... nothing! The ones with- no experience required. O.k. so anyway, you land one of these *fabulous* jobs, cause you're just thankful to be getting a pay check. You bust your ass working (which feels like every day) with an occasional day off thrown in here or there. So, you work and work and work and work... really hard, which I might add, doing everything cause that's the way you are. Till one day you get called to the office, and he says, "I'm sorry. But we have to let you go, because corporate thinks it's best, but, remember if it was up to me, we would keep you on." As he keeps on talking, you've stopped listening at that point, having thoughts like; "I hope this building burns to the ground, hey asshole! Could you have picked a better time?—New year's Day! Happy freaking New Year! What a way to ring in the Holiday... *JOBELESS!* Now you get to go home and tell your kids... "Hey kids, mommy was fired today, how was your day?" *Holy Shit!* Blah, blah, blah, yadda, yadda, yadda! *Can you shut your big fat trap!?* Because this sure isn't the time for reminiscing about whatever the hell you're babbling about! Let me outta here Mac, you are a wasting my time... *Wow...* my, my, my you sure have the gift to gab! I gotta go pound the pavement, unlike *some people* I know!!!!!!!

Carol Mazzei

# BLURB ON A KILLER

What makes a killer kill? Is it for the power, the self-acceptance, or just pure joy? A triumph of saying, "I can take a life at any time, and you can't stop me, only when I allow it." His main concern is how he feels, his own self-pity, his needs and wants... he is the "universe!" So in other words—DON'T FUCK WITH ME!

Some serial killers are caught and others are not, and knowing that they feel superior, so they go out and commit the dastardly crime again and again until they become bored with the game of cat and mouse. Their minds are truly complex, everything to them is hand-crafted, and it's a work of art, a masterpiece... Their very own creation and with that they want to present it to the world. You may ask the question, why do they want to get caught? Well that is when they really and truly become famous. You may also want to ask yourself... Why is there such a fascination about them? A simple answer for that is because we do not understand them, that's why we study and write about them. Still as despicable as they are, they spark an interest in us that we cannot deny. The murders that have taken place throughout time have been gruesome and have been imbedded in our minds forever. There's that intrigue... you know; curiosity. The ability to unleash it all, us writers, psychologists and psychiatrists: We are their light at the end of a tunnel. Without us they are nothing.

In a sense we are just as bad as them, the only difference is we will always have something else we can diagnose or write about besides them. The problem with serial killers is there egos… If it isn't about them, who could it possibly be about? They are always saying some shit… like,

"Someone told me to do it" or "I saw it in a dream… in the music", whatever the fucking case may be, they're lunatics and always will be! It does not matter how many masks they wear, they will always be sought out and found, because if the law doesn't get them, hell will welcome them. There dazzling displays of art; that is what they call it, only what it screams to me is—I am a coward and your lives are mine for the taking. They may go out and commit the crime of the century, but think about it; have they really, or because they know it's wrong, we just assume.

Right about now you might think I am justifying their actions—I couldn't or I would be one of them. I ask you, have you <u>ever</u> thought about killing someone? If you have I guess that makes you a killer. You may argue that to death, but it's true. That's when you would like to crawl inside their minds and seek out what they thrive. Personally I consider it to be clinical bullshit… We are never going to know and never will. Let's face it serial killers are a part of our society and will be until the end of time. Unfortunately we keep them alive by being alive. As long as there are humans walk-ing the earth, there will be killers. We are there salvation, we fascinate them, and our every move intrigues them. How pathetic is that… us being their hobgoblins of life? I think when they are sentenced to life they should make all those useless items you buy at the dollar store.

# SAY IT IN A SONG

People tell me if you really want them to listen say it in a song and just by chance I wrote one while I was listening to "Gimme Some Lovin'" So... O.k. naturally it's going to go with that beat (what the hell kinda sentence did I just write?).

<u>Mother why did you hide my gun?</u>

"Yeah!!
I'm gonna get ya,
I'm gonna get ya,
I'm a comin',
Yeah!!

(Verse 1)

Was it her or was it you that were screwing around?
Well it really doesn't matter cause I'm gonna pound ya down!
I've had it with your lies and your caustic attitude; you're nothing but a crazy psycho loony tune!!

(Chorus)

Mother why did you hide my gun?
Mother why did you hide my gun?
I know, because you knew what you had done.
I know, because you knew what you had done.
Mother give me back my gun right now!

(Verse 2)

I feel so good but not good enough.
Wait until the dark falls and then I'll mess you up, what
you have done your about to lose,
Baby, baby, baby you lose!!

(Chorus)

Mother why did you hide my gun?
Mother why did you hide my gun?
I know, because you knew what you had done.
I know, because you knew what you had done.
Mother give me back my gun right now!
Gimme my gun!

(Verse 3)

Now I'm sittin' in my car watching you run,
I feel like I'm high cause I'm having so much fun,
I shift into gear and I look in the mirror,
I notice there's no cops, so now I'm in the clear!!

(Chorus)

Mother why did you hide my gun?
Mother why did you hide my gun?
I know, because you knew what you had done.
I know, because you knew what you had done.
Mother I don't need my gun no more!!

This is just when the music goes on
and on near the end…

Carol Mazzei

You are soooooooo dead
Splattered
Yeah, yeah
I don't need your love
Yeah
You're gone
Oh happy days
You are soooooooo dead
Bye, bye
I don't need your gun mom
Cause he's dead!
Cause he's dead mom
Yeah
Happy, happy days
He's so dead
I'm soooooooo happy
Outta my life
Happy, happy days
He's so dead
Oh, everyday he's dead
Outta my life!!!"

Wow... I'm good; I could be a songwriter.
Don't ya think? Or not?!

Carol Mazzei

# HELL AND BACK

For the most part someone had told me cats are the best companions to have, far better than children. Let's rephrase that, teenagers!!!! Now when you compare it to that, the choice would definitely be a cat. Listening to experienced parents speak of the horror they went through raising one or even worse.... two or three!! One would say it's like making a choice between living with a man and his ridiculous views on life. Let's face it; men are good for one thing only but half the time not even fucking good at that! I've been around the block a few times to know that's why I can say this and not lie about it. So the simplicities of life shared with a cat results in tranquility one lacks in life...ok, whatever that means. Any who, it is simply outrageous how hectic life can be on any given day. People are born to work, pay bills and raise kids. Then every once and a while if they're lucky, they'll reach that final plateau and have a nervous breakdown just to have some time off. Man oh man, the shit you gotta go through just for a little R & R.

Let me tell you what happened to me, it all started because I hated a man and loved my cats. The journey I'm about to embark you on is a journey of new beginnings and a bitch of a road trip. I remember saying to myself, there is no way in hell I'm going to give up my cats because of some damn man. As far as I'm concerned he can ram his stupid scratched up furniture straight up his ass. Shit, what you do for your cats.

"Corrine don't worry about a thing, my buddy here does

this for a living. That tarp is tied down incredibly tight. It would take a frickin' tornado to blow that sucker off!", shouted Arron. I looked up at my brother standing on top of the one ton truck double checking the load just to be on the safe side.

"Hey thanks Arron, I really appreciate your help". My mind was preoccupied with how I had to drive a half ton pulling a trailer which was also a full load. "Man...you know, if it wasn't for Sam lending me the trucks it would have cost me, I don't know.....a lot. Thanks be the God it's only the gas I have to pay for", I said with a sigh. I took one last look at the house and as I did a flood of memories engulfed me like a bunch of blood thirsty pirates, some good....some bad. It amazed me how quickly nine years have past. "And your sure you don't mine me bringing my son along?" said Arron. "No, of course not it will be fun for him plus it's an extra pair of hands", I said cheerfully. "Did ya see Miss Kitty anywhere, huh did ya," I said frantically. "Hey yeah, I did by the tree, so just calm down, will ya", exclaimed Arron. I walked over and picked her up and placed her carefully on the front seat of the truck. There wasn't much room as the passenger side was packed with boxes, lamps and whatever else wouldn't fit on the truck Arron was driving. The truck had wall to wall carpeting, no wait that was a van I was in 1978. The truck I was driving was in good shape per-say besides the inside of the drivers door had an opening where a speaker once was. Other then that it was in great working order.

I had two other cats but under the circumstances I had left them with my mother and my two kids until I returned the trucks back to Sam. Of all the men I knew Sam was a true friend, I was going to miss him. I choose Miss Kitty because she was due any day now so I wanted to keep a close watch over her, but when you think about it it was kind of a stupid idea. For instance, what if the cat went into labor while driving on the highway on the cramped, dirty floor of the truck? Needless to say we were on our way into a journey we will never forget.

Once we reached the highway I immediately lit a smoke to calm my nerves. I drove behind Arron because it seemed to give me a sense of security. A few years ago I was seconds away from a head on collision driving back from a camping trip. It was I, my younger sister and my two year old daughter. Ever since then I've had a terrible fear of driving on the highway; however, when I do it must be during the day. Cause when the night lays it's cold icy grip upon me I loose all sight. As I sped up to keep up with my brother I could feel the trailer sway from side to side which scared the beJesus out of me. So I had to reduce my speed right the fuck away. At this point I could feel my heart pounding for a fraction of a second I wish I didn't have this idiotic phobia thing! We were no more than eighteen or so kilometers out of the city limits when I noticed the tarp, mother fucking flappin' in the wind. "That didn't take long hey Miss Kitty? Just my shittin' luck. We both pulled over to the shoulder with extreme caution. "Wow.... that lasted a whole five seconds", I exclaimed. "Awwww yeah, I'll fix it, don't sweat it sis", said Arron climbing on top of the truck. As I stood and waited I was just thankful to leave that dead end city and turn over a new leaf. It didn't take Arron long and we were on our way with only one intention: to make it before four O' clock. I automatically lit another smoke and out of the corner of my eye I saw Miss Kitty sleeping comfortably on the blanket I laid down for her. I could feel that damn trailer swaying again, never the less I ignored it the best I could. I came to realize the bloody stupid thing would probably do it all the way there...oh goody! A couple of towns had passed when the tarp was just a givener. Unfortunately this time around it happened to be a little more difficult to fix! "Ok this should hold until we get to Red Deer, our half way point. By the looks of things we are definitely going to need some rope though", Arron explained. "Hey, Arron why not bungee it down and use the rope of course for, you know....double protection", I suggested. Even though it was my brother I felt I had to feed his ego. "That sounds good to me, I'm just a tad bit frustrated cause as it sits right now we're doing really shitty time", Arron expressed. Eric came and stood by us and looked at the god forsaken tarp. "Well so far I'm having a blast....how about you two", Eric asked. I couldn't help but chuckle hysterically at his comment. "And you thought this trip was going to be boring, shame on you", I said shaking my head. Eric was a great kid, easy to get along with and for a twelve year old he was quit tall. I guess that's only natural he is the spitting image of his father.

We all went back to our vehicles thinking this couldn't possibly get any worse. In spite of it all, it was a gorgeous day not a cloud in the sky, blue as far as the eye could see. Before I continued the drive I checked Miss Kitty who was still curled up asleep. A smile spread across my lips just looking at her inflicted me with serenity. As I drove I thought of how well my kids were going to adjust to a new city and tackle new schools and so on. Actually, they did express their views on the whole thing which went something like this..... "It's gonna suck, I'm never going to have any friends, the schools there are stupid, what kinda clothes do they wear there?" So with that in mind I knew it was a huge adjustment for them. Not only for them, but for myself also. I was leaving the one person I loved and cared about; my sister Julie.

So being preoccupied in thought I didn't notice that it had started to rain. Turning on my windshield wipers I glimpsed at the truck this time the tarp was worse then ever.

Shit....it looked like that fucker was going to take flight! We turned onto a dirt road having a very strong feeling this time it would take longer to strap down. "Can you believe this..... I mean look at it it's freakin' pouring!", Arron shouted. "Yes.....as a matter-of-fact I can," I responded. Standing there shivering waiting to see if he needed my help but he seemed to be handling it so I ran back to the truck and grabbed my only jacket. I brought it along to plug the speaker hole so Miss Kitty wouldn't go back in there, as she almost didn't make it out of the damn door the first time. What a crazy time this was, I mean my life had always been complicated yet simple all-in-one. If that was even possible. With the rain dripping in my eyes I glanced up and heard Arron cursing as he fought with the tarp once again. As I watched my bother struggle with the damn thing I started to laugh and what made me laugh even more was I could hear Eric swearing his head off in the cab of the truck. Overwhelmed with what was happening I didn't realize how soaked I was. For some particular reason I dashed back to the truck cause I had a strange feeling about Miss Kitty and as sure as shit she crawled into that confounded hole. I called out to her hoping she would come out. Why....why.....why I thought to myself she was definitely stuck in that fucking, god damn mother fucking door! I called for her again but she wouldn't budge. I tried to stay calm so my poor cat wouldn't pick up my extreme sense of frustration. Not saying a word I could see she was making an effort to back her way out; considering that would be her only exit. I mean it's not like she could just turn around she was to bloody pregnant. By this time I was becoming frantic thinking my god I won't be able to get her out, she will die!!! I pleaded for her to come out as the tears were streaming down my face not to mention I was soaked to the skin. Meanwhile in the distance Arron was swearing like there was no fucking tomorrow because the tarp was just not cooperating. Or maybe it had something to do with the wind factor...I don't know but all I knew was I had to get her out of there before I lost my mind. The unfortunate thing about my final decision was that it would, without a doubt hurt her beyond anything she's ever experienced. I was compellingly torn for what was going to happen next. "I know this is going to hurt Miss Kitty you have left me no choice", I said sobbing uncontrollably. Grabbing her by her hind legs I hesitated a moment then I began to pull. I could feel her fighting me and I know in my heart if I didn't do this she....would....die. As I continued to pull, her swollen pregnant belly scraped across the jagged metal and she meowed in pain. Nevertheless after much distress I got her out. My first instinct was to check if she was seriously injured on her delicate fragile body. To my relief she was fine. I held her in my arms, cradling her and speaking softly, comforting her. She sensed my grief and started to purr. With that ordeal over I placed her on the seat and peeled off my jacket then stuffed it back into that damn hole. Arron ran over towards me curious about what just took place. "M-i-s-s K-i-t-t-y, M-i-s-s K-i-t-t-y, s-s-she's safe...now!" Arron hugged me because he could feel my pain and asked if I was okay to drive. I assured him I was cool, and we continued our journey with the hopes the worst was over.

The rain persisted for a few more kilometers then finally let up. As I lit a smoke, I heard a horn. I looked through my rear view mirror but no one was behind me. The honking continued it was the car beside me, the driver was trying to tell me something. Under the circumstances how was I to understand, driving ninety five kilometers an hour. He rolled down his window. as did I, yelling at the top of his lungs. "You're loosing some of your load!" Concentrating on staying on the road, "What....!" I shouted. "You are loosing things off your load", he screamed. I signaled that I got the picture and pulled on to the shoulder. I got out and leaned against the truck waiting for Arron to notice I was no longer behind him and at that rate we were going, it wouldn't take long at all for him to notice. I kept telling myself it would be nice to get there before night fall. Arron sauntered towards me slowly removing his sunglasses. "So.....what's up now sis", he said with a smirk. "Well....apparently some of my belongings are scattered on the highway". "Ya know....somehow that doesn't surprise me, come to think of it nothing does any more", said Arron. I rubbed my forehead, "I don't know about you big brother but I'm fucking exhausted". "Hang in there girl not all hope is lost....yet", he assured. Don't get me wrong it takes a little more than these mishaps to make me suicidal. I'm not weak or feeble by any means, unlike my parents and I vowed I would never follow in their footsteps. Oh.....but I curse that saying never say never. Arron assured me once again that it would stay secure until we reached Red Deer but if my memory serves me correctly he said that before.

Thank god our stop in Red Deer was a brief one just long enough to secure both loads cause it was literally turning out to look like something off a 1-800-junk truck.....holy crap. Naturally though we ended up pulling over one last time for the "you-know-what" before we entered Edmonton City limits. I have to say the thing that pissed me off the most was the help we had to unload the furniture was naturally no longer available because by the time we arrived it was seven forty five PM......oh gee, when did we leave..... Noon!!!!

I apologized profusely to my friend, Karen who had arranged the help for us. I told her every shitty thing that happened. I could see in her face she was trying not to laugh but she burst into laughter and I along with her. By that point sleep was the only thing on my mind. The morning came too soon for my liking on the other hand I wanted this over in the worst way. I gave the landlord a call to meet us there with the key. She said she would be at least an hour, in the mean time we waited, Karen offered us something to eat. At least that gave us some time to do some catching up. "Karen thanks a lot for everything I'll see you when I get back". "That's for sure but in the meantime you two take it easy driving back....ok. It was nice meeting you Arron and Eric keep an eye on them", Karen said with a wink. Eric smiled shyly at her comment and nodded.

Unloading was nothing but pure hell to say the least and for our organizational skills....well they sucked! I mean whoever designed this crummy townhouse had to have been on crack, smack, coke or whatever cause each room was on it's own level. Stairs then the kitchen then another set of stairs to the living room and freakin' so on. By the time we were done I thought....this is it, we're dead. Ultimately every muscle in my body throbbed in pain. As I fought with my inner self, I must go on-I must go on. Arron looked at me as if I was some kind of lunatic. "How are you for fuel", he asked. "I should be fine at least until we get to the half way mark.... I think....I hope", I trailed off. "Well then we'd better hustle if we want to make it back before dark", Arron remarked. "Yes....before dark....we can't let it get dark....not dark....no-it can't happen", I said with a distinct sound of lunacy. Arron sensed hysterics in my voice so with that said we systematically got in our trucks and headed back onto the dreaded hell bound highway.

I eyed my gas gauge like a hawk watching it move closer and closer to the empty mark. The more I watched the more incredibly nervous I became, just praying I wouldn't run out of gas because the way my luck was going there was a good chance of it happening. There was one thing not to worry about any more....that infernal tarp. Up ahead was my salvation- Gas Land Alley which for the first time in my life

I truly appreciated a gas station. "Honest to God Arron I didn't think I was going to make it". "Well you did so the worst is over right....right", he said nudging me playfully. "One more hour and I can have a relaxing hot shower, good God my clothes are freakin' filthy and my hair....oh yuck I feel gross!", I ranted.

Excited to be on my way to that orgasmic shower I glanced at the gas gauge and it wasn't moving, panic enveloped all around me. Arron assured me it wasn't broken so with that in mind I convinced myself of his ridiculous theory. I knew I had to drive like a demon before darkness engulfed the winding road. It was no more than one hundred meters or so when, yeah....that's right, the truck died. I tried starting it but it was utterly hopeless; this thing wasn't going anywhere and Arron was long gone. At that moment I happened to remember that Sam kept a gun in the glove compartment and then I remembered he also told me about the switch to change the tanks over. I thought switch-gun, switch-gun, nay better go for the switch. A ray of hope shined upon me, reaching to flip it I chanted, "Don't let me down now, make mama happy...Son of a bitch, nothings fucking happening!" I gripped the steering wheel feeling nothing but utter despair and helplessness. I gazed out the windshield as tears welled up in my eyes. I didn't know what the hell I was going to do because I spent my last fucking cent on gas for a truck that doesn't work!! Uncontrollably I began to cry, knowing I was doomed I still hoped Arron would notice something missing....me! My head dropped to the steering wheel as I sobbed. By this time darkness surrounded me like a pack hungry wolves waiting to devour me. Yes....it was true I was at the end of my rope and that gun was starting to look good now but on the other hand I was scared shitless all at the same time. All I heard myself say why....why....why, it's not fair I've worked so damn hard. You know the whole self pity trip. I looked up trying to pull myself together in case Arron by some miracle was on his way back probably wondering what the hell happened now! He pulled in behind me and both of them came merrily to greet me. I'm being sarcastic of course. "I'm really beginning to wonder Corrine if it is worth it. I don't mean to sound pessimistic but I'll have to admit this has been quite a.....how do I put it, a hell and back adventure", said Arron. "I know life sucks but I rather it not end here". "What's the damage", Arron enquired. "I'm pretty sure it's the stupid piece of shit switch." "I don't know about you but I have an incredible urge to take a sludge hammer and just giver until this thing is in a billion pieces", he said psychotically. "Dad are you alright?", said Eric lightly, not sure if he should have said anything at all. "I'm fine son, I was releasing a little repressed anger that one gets when faced with one hundred and one catastrophes right after the other. But hey....I'm ok....really." Eric and I stood in silence with our mouths open, waiting for more outlandish outbursts by our faithful host. But that was it....he was done, thank god! "We have to get it towed back to the gas station, are you a member with the AMA cause I'm not?", I asked apprehensively. "I read in the Enquirer once about a couple who moved to Cleveland and a similar incidence occurred, but on top of it all they were robbed then left in the middle of nowhere and as I read on they finally ended up in straight jackets in an asylum somewhere", Eric trailed off. "I have this feeling we won't be that lucky my dear nephew that would mean our agony we're dealing with would end." Arron and I burst into laughter at Eric's crazy story. "Can you two pull yourselves together so we can get home? I would like it if we could do that.....go home, maybe something crazy like eat", Eric ranted. We slowly brought our laughter to a halt and tried to be serious for Eric's sake. As we walked Eric told us more stories that we couldn't help but laugh about I guess it made it more bearable to contend with. Arron made his call to the AMA and called his wife to tell her that they would be home a little later than expected. "Did you guys notice this phone booth has a seat in it, I guess for those weird people who really like to gab", Eric announced. "That's funny Eric I can picture it now someone sitting there chatting about whatever", I answered. Arron saw the tow truck and started walking towards it. "Oh thank God they are here. You two stay here and I'll go and while I'm gone see if you can stay out of trouble", said Arron. "Yes sir", we saluted.

I looked over at Eric with sort of a painful blank look....if that's possible. "I'm starved how about you?" Eric asked. "I know what you mean; if I don't eat I think I might pass out. As soon as you dad gets back we'll grab a bite."

They sat back in their chairs drinking their pop feeling a great sense of satisfaction from filling their appetites. Arron leaned across the table like he was going to confess his sin or something. "I believe this was a sign from God." I frowned at his ridiculous statement. "No no, I don't mean about anything that has happened just concerning the truck." I was trying to figure out what he was saying then it hit me, my fear of driving on the highway in the dark. "I believe you are right because even if nothing had gone wrong we wouldn't have made it back before dark anyway. What I'm about to say may sound sick and twisted, but I'm glad this happened. Who knows I could be dead right now", I said. "So I take it you are ok riding with me then?" Arron asked. "Not a doubt in my mind, knowing I'll get back in one piece is a load off my mind."

The two hour ride back was superbly glorious considering how totally burnt out we all were and I was dreading tomorrow having to tell Sam about his truck. "Corrine, the next time you want to move do us all a favor.....call professional movers", he said jokingly. That was pretty damn funny I had to admit, at this point we were allowed to laugh about it cause it was over....for now until my return trip to my new city but that's a whole different story.

☺

Smoking is cool ... isn't it!? Taking that cigarette out of the pack then placing it between your lips. Knowing that any second all your worries and cares will disappear. Think about it ... just that sensation alone is worth living for!!!! Life is sooooo much better now that you lit that cigarette????! But at the same time you question yourself... don't ya! It just isn't putting it between your lips... it's the way you put it between your lips that counts! Ahhh... the satisfaction... there's nothing like, not even sex!!!! Nothing can take the place of a cigarette.... right?! When you think about it everything goes with a cigarette... coffee... before a meal, after a meal, waiting for the bus, driving your car, on the computer, talking on the phone, not talking on the phone, watching a movie, listening to music, dancing to music, before exercising, after exercising, while you're cooking, before you start to cook, writing, associating with your friends or people you can't stand, cleaning, before you start to clean, drinking a beer, before sex, after sex, even when you're on the verge of a nervous breakdown, lost in the woods, being told you have a week to live, broke down on the highway in the middle of nowhere, when a wasp lands on your ass, fed up with your job, your boss, your bills, not qualifying for GST, hiding from a madman... the list is endless. LIGHT THAT CIGARETTE... 'CAUSE IT MAY BE YOUR LAST!!!!!!!!!

☺

Carol Mazzei

Centuries ago when a man in Asia sat down and thought of how he could please all of his concubines because he knew damn well he sure as to hell couldn't and plus knowing he... himself had a weenie the size of a toothpick. So he researched what an average American male penis looks like he then made an exact duplicate from the pictures he saw. From there he put it to the test... handing the magnificent ten inch love-muscle to each of his concubines. He then began to describe in much detail what he wanted his beauties to do and as he did he noticed a look of terror in their eyes. In order for his invention to work he had to reassure his women not to fear it but to embrace it and feel the ultimate pleasure of its intentions. As he watched his women reeling themselves threw multiple orgasms he wished it was him bringing them such erotic sensual rapture. The moans he heard, of pleasure, slowly dissipated as well as his own from jerking off repeatedly... there was something he didn't realize... he had just replaced the only thing he had going for him... his cock! And they say men are the masterminds of the universe... yeah... the masterminds of fucking themselves over.

Ninety nine percent of the time life is cruel

and the other one percent is resentment.

When right out of the blue a crazy person happens to you call you up one day and tells you a bunch of shit… don't panic… just take a deep breathe and pick up the complete works from Edger Allan Poe and start reciting " The Raven" 'cause you know how long it is and most crazy people have A.D.D to begin with. So the good thing about it… you won't have to read  the whole thing! Oh yeah… and most crazies are insect people. Also a smart thing to do is keep that double gauge shotgun by your door just in case you hear a sudden tapping, rapping, rapping at your chamber door.

Carol Mazzei

See 1stWorld Books at:

www.1stWorldPublishing.com

See our classic collection at:

www.1stWorldLibrary.org